AFTERLIFE

First published in 2010 by
The Dedalus Press
13 Moyclare Road
Baldoyle
Dublin 13
Ireland

www.dedaluspress.com

ISBN 978 1 906614 20 1

Dedalus Press titles are represented in North America by
Syracuse University Press, Inc., 621 Skytop Road,
Suite 110, Syracuse, New York 13244,
and in the UK by
Central Books, 99 Wallis Road, London E9 5LN

Cover image: Casa de Mateus, Portugal © Pat Boran

The Dedalus Press receives financial assistance from
The Arts Council / An Chomhairle Ealaíon

AFTERLIFE

Pádraig J. Daly

DEDALUS PRESS
DUBLIN, IRELAND

For Paul, Marc, Ian and Odhrán

Contents

Time of Peace

It is evening
And swallows invade the sky over our streets.
The old man moves fruitboxes indoors,
Begins to sort the rotten from the good.
A woman emerges with a knot of onions,
Places them on the ground beside a russet cardigan.
In accustomed unison, they fold away their day.

A girl arrives for a final purchase,
Is quickly, breathlessly, gone.
The man locks the door,
Stoops for a rollaway potato.
The woman stands,
Looking disinterestedly towards the swooping birds.
The man retrieves a car, returns.

She enters, turns to him and smiles.
Together they vanish into enfolding night.

Couple

Nowadays he spends all his time
In the garden,
Digging, hoeing,
Drowning his aubergines
In water.

She watches him from the window,
Loving him more
Than when first he came,
Young and beautiful,
Bounding to her over the mountains.

Passenger

She is taking the train
To visit her sister
In the high blocks
Outside the city,
Smiling for happiness.

She is bringing biscuits
Wrapped with ribbon,
A block of marzipan,
A blouse she bought
And never wore.

Her husband sits beside her,
Older than herself,
Beginning to forget.
He will tire early
Of the sisterly chatter,

Fall asleep,
Looking out on the cleft
In the mountain,
Sun-scorched grass,
Green bed of a vanished stream.

Milkwoman

She comes uphill into the village
Just before morning,
Dressed in mourner's black,
Carrying silvery buckets.

She fills the waiting jugs with warm milk,
Covers them with lids and saucers,
Chattering all the while to drowsy cats,
Sparing them dribbles.

Toil done,
She descends again the shaly path
Through vine and olive
Into transfiguring dawn.

Pause

A church with majolica dome,
A soldier on a plinth,
Weary after his war;

A girl running, losing a heel,
A dog chasing pigeons from a tree,
Stalky oleander.

Away on the hills,
Smallholdings needing rain.

Do not forget the shale by the track,
Blue bindweed,
Somebody, carefree, whistling.

Christmas Poem

Crenellated buildings sparkle in the sun.
There is frost in the air
But no breeze.
Shepherds are in from the hills,
Playing ancient carols.

As night falls, small lights come on
One after another.
The stars burn in the sky.
And we are touched once more
By something perfect, certain, beyond our busynesss.

Sadhbh, Aged 4

You have taken to wearing dresses,
Pale, light as mothwing,
Long enough to trip on.

You race and run all day
And gather marbly pebbles
And flee from spiders.

We hear you laugh from the meadow
As if the whole bright world we live in
Were a bauble for your pleasure.

Sadhbh, Aged 5

A swan today,
In a secluded corner of the lake,
Lifted its wings in the sun
Till the tips of its feathers
Disappeared in light;
It folded then its head
Into its downy breast,
Peeping slyly:

Reminding me of how bright sun
Plays colourgames with your hair as you race;
And then, the stop,
Remembering to be shy,
To find a skirt or pillow
To hide your face in
And peep at the attending world
With mirthful eye.

Flower Girl

Sadhbh, at five and a bit

She walks the long passage,
Flowers in her hair,
Aware of all the eyes upon her.

Small flickers of bliss
Move across her solemn face.
She goes from shy to confident

And back again.
She longs to run to her tall father,
Be lifted into sky;

But duty and joy
Dictate
This measured pace.

First Communions

"The whole of our faith is the belief that God loves us: I mean there just isn't anything else. Anything else we say we believe is just a way of saying that God loves us."
—Herbert McCabe O. P.

Let the enchantment commence:

Deck the boys in slick suits,
Gel their hair.

Fit the girls out in petticoated frocks,
Pin cloth roses on their tresses.

Teach them to join hands,
Walk an aisle decorously.

Can it matter,
In God's enormity,

That few who watch,
Aglow in the light of a child,

Know the why of the bread,
Have any prayer but, "Thanks"?

Country Children, Christmas

Coming only rarely to town,
In ponderous buses,
They thought our everyday wonderful:

Water swirling and swishing in toilet bowls, gushing taps,
Christmas lights, toy tractors, whining police-cars,
Dolls with eyelids that opened and shut.

We watched them move through the ordinary,
Eyes feverish with delight.

Jake, Before His Birth

22 November 2006

You come when squirrels
Are finishing their forage for Winter,
When the last leaves wait
To be shaken from the trees;
And we are all-fearful, all-happy
As we imagine
Your tiny newness on the earth.

When rivers fill again
With racing water,
And crows return soon
To their branches,
When the holly is sending
An early berry out,
You are Christmas before Advent dark.

Óisín, Aged 1

When I doubt Love,
I think of you,
All wobbly-bellied,
Banging a rattle
Noisily against your chair;

Staring first
At your face's replica,
Then whipping glasses
Suddenly off a nose,
Flinging them exuberantly to floor;

Stretching arms and legs
As though to reach
The very tip of the space
Your lengthening limbs
Will one day occupy;

Chuckling,
As if you knew
That the tale of humankind
Has a merry ending.

Sophie

1. BEFORE HER BIRTH

Into the Christmas chaos,
Your soon-coming is announced.

And your mother,
Standing tall and lovely in a modish dress,

Is no longer another such
But a bearer of miracle.

2. AT 18 MONTHS

You wake crying.
The pond outside your window
Is covered in ice.

There is snow on the roadway,
In the fields,
On the trees.

A wild goose calls out in distress.
Your father comes from sleep
To lift and comfort you.

Liam Michael

30.10.2008

We had hailstones
The day you were born,
Covering the ground like cherryblossom.

Then the air grew warm;
And they were water,
Racing downhill in gleeful rivulets.

For Juliette

1.

AT THREE DAYS

Some day you will open wide those eyes,
Put long legs down,
Fill the house with merry tumult.

But now, confused by free-range limbs,
You are wrapped like a cosied egg;
And nothing fierce or fearsome disturbs your slumber.

2.

You are to our lives
Like those windfalls of childhood,
Peeping, ruddy and cheerful, out of high grasses
When Autumn rains were spent,
Juicier and sweeter
Than the brightest fruit on the branch.

Let Us Adore The Lord

from the Irish, 11th century

Let us adore the Lord,
Creator of wonders:
Bright heaven with its angels,
The whitecapped sea below.

In Prayer

1.

The "Why are we?" has no answer
Except to sit in bareness before Mystery,
Feel again
The tender numbering of our hairs.

2.

Whatever God is,
He cannot be All-Other.
He is ever about us, interbound in our sighs,
Gently sifting the waste of our days.

3.

From Whom All Comes,
I wait,
Plunged into the terrifying naught of self,
Crying, "Mercy!"

4.

Why did God create us in our throngs,
Dividing, coalescing,
Loving our own selves beyond all others?
What is the point of us?

5.

Our unquiet minds
Scrape like hens' legs
In the soil
Of the Unfathomable.

6.

We who have but the fish and bread
Of age and unbelief,
Give them to You, Lord,
To feed the dreamless multitude.

7.

Deep into her prayer she carried him;
And jealously he watched her
Sit before the What or Who,
Her soul plunging seas beyond him.

8.

Without and Other, your fingers brush our faces,
Not where we seek You in soulful earnestness,
But in the shabby places where we love,
The snow territories of desolation.

9.

Rublev painted a white space
Amid the Trinity of Angels
To show the emptiness God in God makes
For our scatterhearted love to fill.

10.

And sometimes God drops a feather
On the floor of a tossed-about life,
Showing, against obviousness,
That we are wrapped in benignity.

Planter

from the Irish of Giolla Bríde Ó hEódhusa, 16th century

You who plant the tree,
Will you live to see the apple?
When the branches grow and spread,
That you will view them, is it certain?

You may be gone before it flowers
In the green and lovely orchard.
Consider as you fix the stake,
That that is often how things happen.

Should the fruit of those bright branches
Ripen; and your hand enclose it,
Will you eat it, sweet companion?
Death makes such an outcome doubtful.

You show little wisdom, Sir,
You who own the fragrant woodland,
To place your hope on paltry crop
And never make your soul your worry.

Train

Where does the train go,
Rattling noisily through the valley?
Already darkness encloses it,
Its windows—for how long?—filled with brittle light.

The Poem of Mary, Queen of The Heavens

from the Irish of Tadhg Gaelach Ó Súilleabháin, 18ᵗʰ century

Queen of the Heavens,
You are my warning staff,
My tender counsellor:
I am under your shelter.

It is my intent and my decision,
If I live a thousand years,
My swift Courageous Empress,
That I never shift from you.

Small wonder I love you,
Blessed, Crystal Candle,
Nurse and Gracious Mother
Of the True Son, who bought us dearly.

Radiant Light of Heaven's City,
Ask again in prayerful charity,
Of your darling Son, that our greed
And accursedness be forgotten

On that terrible day, that slaughterous day, that day of burning,
The day the villains are condemned, the day of terror,
The dreadful day in which the damned are separated
From the beloved sorority of the Prince of Heaven.

For the privilege beyond all God's children,
The love your Child holds for you,
Had I all the sins of Eva's race upon me,
Your Heir, Your Beauty, would forgive them for you.

On your own account call me near you
In that citadel of song, of saints, of angels,
To regally, lavishly, preciously, psalmingly,
Praise Him forever and ever and ever.

Queen of Friday, Queen of Saturday,
Show me that path I never yet travelled,
Guide me faithfully and directly
As the star guided the eastern magi.

Draw me up in your nets
To the harbour of light
Where the merry virgins and martyrs
Dwell, who in their deeds followed Christ;

The gorgeous happy patriarchs thronging,
The apostles and blessed fathers,
The highest, holiest, most fortunate confessors
And theology's honoured, golden doctors;

The virtuous prophets, full of vigour,
The saints of Ireland lustily Te Deum-ing,
And that glorious patriarch, Blessed Joseph,
As a tuneful, powerful general, leading.

There's no pain or sorrow, night or day,
No tear or gloom on those wise faces.
I am moved to laughter by their exuberance
As they praise untiringly the noble Trinity
.

All this band share a sunlit bower,
A bower of light without spite or rancour,
A bower beyond all bowers earthly,
The palace of the lovely ones of the kingdom of heaven.

There they find solace beyond solace,
There is ease, all ease surpassing,
There is mercy, glory, blessedness
For the fragrant band of the courts of Jesus.

It is there that the queen beyond queens, our shelter,
The lady beyond ladies, our darling,
The virgin of virgins, our sweetness,
Above them all as a star is shining.

Ask, all of you, that this prayer be heard,
Through the loving afflictions of the mother of Christ:
By the power of your death and passion, Jesus,
Take my soul as a pearl to your merry realm.

Saviour, give this alms to your people,
Whom You bought so dearly by your blood and passion:
Pity us, O Faithful Deliverer,
Heart of Generosity, bring us to your kingdom.

Jansenists

Afflicted themselves,
Our teachers taught us
To place ourselves hereafter,
Not along the chalk avenues of hope,
But, faultfilled, among the rejected,
Moving uncompanionably towards eternal mayhem.

If death, then, were a wall
With nothing, not even emptiness,
Beyond, if life might stop
Without the fuss of a forever,
Our trepid hearts would surge
In gratitude.

Fear

It is not death itself
But the before
That we fear:

Decay preceding decay,
Winter of the heart,
The falling-in of flesh,

Drawn-out pain
In narrow beds,
The mind losing its edge,

Losing its self,
The worm feeding
On the pus of being.

In Those Times

Every act had eternal consequence:

We lived in a world, bigger,
Not with angels and dreams of Paradise,

But with the fear
That God would gather us,
Like crumbs into a dustpan,

And pitch us forever
Onto the hot furnaces of hell.

Forever

The "forever" flummoxes us:

The bliss of belovedness,
The ecstasy of the bike-hurtle
Down the hill,
Of limbs through water,
Lift us for a moment only.

How can we,
Who have never known
A permanence,
Grasp joy without drear,
A lasting now of delight?

Purgatory

1.

The "I" then
Is a freed dove,
Flapping for a moment
Against the beams of its confinement,

Hesitant,
As, all fault,
It looks to its mark
And dares not fly.

2.

Must we still believe
That after death
Our sins follow us
And we find ourselves
In a barren place,
Aching unbearably for God?

Or what of the farmer,
We read about in our book,
Espying his son afar,
Running, even in age,
To clasp him tenderly home.

Platonist

1.

Rounding another corner, hurrying,
There where the street breaks,
I am halted by a wide river,
Brown and gold and full of sun.

And I weep,
Not for joy or sorrow
Or buried loss,
But for the perfection such beauty harbinges.

2.

The young were coming festively
Into the sun.
The day was without cloud.

Outside the church,
One, more beautiful,
Embraced me;

And on I walked, naked on the steppes,
Hungry for the caress
That would hold me forever.

Canal Bank

The rain has cleared the air
And now the sun
Drenches an outstretched line of water,

Touches white cloths on a table
Where a couple eat late breakfast,
The verge, where an excited girl feeds moorhens.

What fuller joy can paradise provide?

Moment

They were closing the doors of the cathedral.
The singers had gone.

Outside it was an evening
Of warm breezes and moonlight.

People sat on the steps,
Heads full of music,

Caught into a moment
Without past or tomorrow.

Imaging an Afterlife

"We must not smuggle in the idea that we can throw the analogy away and, as it were, get behind it to a purely literal truth. Freedom from a given metaphor is often only freedom to choose between that metaphor and others."
—C.S. Lewis, "Letters to Malcolm"

1.

Year on year,
From all corners
And all on foot,
We wend towards the high walls
That loom above the plains of our joy.

Night falls as we near.
The stone is dark,
The entries narrow.

But within,
Unknown,
The squares are lit,
People feast and dance
Along the thoroughfares
Of requited hope.

2.

Through a narrow aperture
And then into a broad courtyard,

The arches airy and high,
Looking onto roses.

At the far corner,
A doorway, drawing us towards Light

And the Now that swallows
All our tearful nows.

3.

He came stumbling into the village,
Fearful,
Empty rifle uselessly ready.

Fledgling sparrows rose and dropped,
Dropped and rose.
He smelt fresh bread and jasmine.

Festive bunting proclaimed the peace.
People emerged to welcome him,
New come to this place,

Knowing it as home.

4.

Yes, we will know one another then;
And each of us will glow with God,
Our finitude grown infinite.

5.

She came through the doors
Diffidently.
Nothing had prepared her

For the burst of light,
The mirthful throng,
Her weary feet abandoning shoes to dance.

6.

You will come first
To the region of storms and icy precipices.
Do not fear.
You will not be alone in the wind.

Next you will reach
The valley of waking birds,
Roam its outspread fields,
Intoxicated by the exhalations of grasses.

Beyond you,
The sun will lift itself out of the sea.
Walk towards the sun
Until you are a speck in its circling flame.

7.

Like some glorious insects
Drying their mucoid wings,
We wake into light.

8.

By a wall of the ruined farmhouse,
He found a single horse,
Waiting diffidently.

They made sure way
Along a road grown over
With grass and hurrying vetch,

Onto pathways
That hung vertiginously
Above the sea,

Resting to watch
Random sun
Turn gold a shingle beach,

Towards that last haven
Where painted houses
Sparkled above the water.

9.

There is a photo missing
From the album of her life:
The Lord God reaching
And lifting her to light.

10.

The sun was shining.
We rowed, without strain,
Out to the middle of the lake.

A dog barked.
A grey heron went by.
We breathed the fresh scents of morning.

Mist came down comfortingly.
The old unwound their limbs.
The young exulted in their lissomness.

We could hear voices,
Preparing our welcome.

11.

All his years he spent
And all his strength
Ploughing heather upland;

Edging stones out of the turf,
Digging to the roots of the furze,
Building dry walls, excavating ditches.

Now he stands
Before the gates of the city,
The Long-Absent moving to him out of light,

Towels on His shoulder,
Carrying a bowl for his feet.

12.

Out we came,
As from water into air.
Our gnarled carapaces fell aside.

Love no longer found resistance
And flowed like an unguent
Over our needy skin.

13.

He entered the house of many rooms:
Some opening onto lawns sweeping to a river,
Others onto blue mountains.

One hung
Above a stormy inlet of the sea,
Another looked tranquilly on a bridge.

One was empty of everything,
Another teemed with ancient friends.
Rooms there were for all delight,

Sanctums for battered hearts.

14.

The son falls heavily into his father's arms,
Babbling about offence, regret,
Speaking to lance his suppurating soul.

The father holds him hard against himself
(Between them now, tsunamis of tears),
Lifts a finger, gives command.

Water is brought, robes for his skin.
Tables are laid with honeycakes.
The smell of veal fills lusciously the air.

15.

Death will lead us then, tenderly,
Beyond the glowering walls,
The grilled apertures,
The back and forward of our enclosure,

Into a land of fresh sun
With horses galloping unfettered
Out into unending meadows.

16.

Perhaps it is that good dream
When toil and tears,
Recurring misery,
Festering absences
Are put aside
And we rub our half-awaking eyes
In a temperate garden by the sea.

Perhaps it is that moment
When those we love are about us
Without rancour and forever;

And this mind,
Which ranges wildly now
The vast world and the spheres,
Rests like a martin
In a cleft of the divine.

Who

Who speak in the tints of sky,
The lift of a bird,
I do not know You,

Who are solid and real
Whenever my fingers reach
Clumsily to comfort,

Who live in every love
By which I ever am loved,
Whom I follow,

Through the hosannas
And the supper,
Out to the desolate garden,

Whom I trust
Through the portcullises
Of my end.

Knowing

We know how stars divide,
How atoms race and run,
How the first explosion
Sent planets hurtling,
How there is a maw in the spheres,
Lurking to swallow everything;

And miss the small perfection
Of bird alighting,
Dilettante butterfly,
The oak over the river
Sheltering the sensitive fish;

And sometimes
If we fold ourselves
Into that quiet and wait,
The Other comes,
Touching us with madness
And certitude.

Virginal States

1.

In this new land,
Where a million flowers bloom showily
And the fancy of a night
Leads blithely to the actions of love,

A virgin heart is an awkward thing,
Its hurts and longings unaccountable.

2.

Like strips of cloth
On thorntrees at a well,
My torn heart.

3.

Love left behind in the wedding hall rejoicing,
I drive through lanes
Flamboyant with whitethorn and lady lace,
Nursing a vague, insistent hurt,

My skin yearning for touch,
My heart a snow keep
Above the passes of Summer.

4.

There is no time any longer for preludes:
Descriptions of savage roots
Twisting iron rails out of shape,
Rain on black streets,
Gaunt elms.

I have but one theme:
My body – poor foolish body -
Calling, not for any human touch,
But for God;
And His dereliction of me.

Psalm

My prayers are made in faith,
Without feeling,
Aware but coldly
That You are above, below,
About, within.

You lift me no longer
Into the warm realms of delight.
I have forgotten all my joy.
I walk a track by a grey river,
Knowing I must plod monotonously on.

Reading in Mark

Yesterday a tractor turned the green sward black.
Today I draw my drapes
On a world made white by frost.

All morning I have been reading in Mark
Of the man they lowered to Jesus through a roof.
I am weary

Of relentless days among the sorrowful;
And would yield gladly
To those who would lower me to be touched.

The Little Sister

i.m. Agnes Gonxha Bojaxhiu, Mother Teresa

1.

Beyond where mind can go,
You lured her,
Into trust,

Brushing fleetingly her skin,
Filling her senses
With savour.

But now
You bombard her with ice;
Her heart is frozen over.

Knowing You unfeelingly,
She is sent
Among the clamouring unfed.

2.

A limewashed platform
Rises above the track.
The rails run off to empty horizon.
It is a Summer place
After the crowds have gone.
No trains come.
No trains go.

I will be, she said,
If God is kind,
A saint of darkness,
Uneasy, even in my heaven,
When day is done
And the landscape of hearts
Is arid-scoured with lime.

Pattern

The sun shines on the white walls of the ruined chapel,
On sinuous Eve and Adam beneath their tree,
On the carved Magi bringing gifts to the Virgin.

Beyond,
The wind-tormented sea
Sends out morses of light.

On the rocky outcrop,
Where Deuglán made his desert,
Where Tadhg circled with his cuallacht of women,

A crowd circles again;
And the bleak gulls, echoing in the crevices of the cliff,
Carry their agonies into God.

In the Light of "Ryan"

1.

They came together, as we did,
In draughty chapels,
Offering their weakness,
Praying, as we did,
For light.

How did You not, Lord,
Listen?

2.

In our story,
We imagined ourselves
Facing fire and anger staunchly
In cause of gentleness.

Never did we number ourselves
Amid the afflicters.

3.

Besides the sin
That is my own sin,
That old sin of origin
Runs raw on the flesh of our humanity.

4.

We huddle in our upper room,
The doors bolted,
For shame at our betrayal
Of all that is tender.

To our place of infamy, come,
Jesus, come.

Christmas 2009: After "Murphy"

Let us take the figure of the buried Christ
Out of the storerooms and undercrofts,
Brush the cobwebs off,
Carry it through the streets
To sound of wailing,

Past taverns and coffeehouses,
Up escalators,
Under arches.
Let santas and snowmen gape,
Let mechanical elves pause in their labour.

In the manger of the Child,
Before the awed shepherds,
Let us lay Him.

Winter

for Daniel, when he is fifty; and in memory of Mary C.

The city wakes to snow hardening into ice.
People pick their way to the buses.

All night I have been following
Furrowed pathways of the mind—

God or emptiness?
God kind or God indifferent?

Longing for an atheist faith,
A godless certainty,

Till I am stopped again
By images of love:

A sick woman reaching out of pain,
A child's smile like a sacrament.

Institution

White goalposts
Rise out of the long grasses
Of the seminary fields.

The house is empty
Save for the shuffling few,
Astray along its shabby corridors,

Remembering thump of ball
Crack of sliotar,
Yelp and counteryelp.

The proud façade crumbles in the wind.
The roof lets water in.
The grass edges to the door.

Chapel

When we are gone and our lives are mystery,
Children will find this place
And wonder at its steps and spaces;

Roofbeams aspiring to sky,
Slabs of broken marble,
Leaves scraping underfoot,

Carcasses of birds,
Sleeping butterflies,
Hushed echoes of prayer.

Room

I always wanted to sleep
In that room that rose like a watchtower
Above the valley,
Listening to insects click their wings
And figs fall lusciously into bushes.

I recall the dun walls,
Stained with the corpses of slaughtered mosquitoes,
Rickety washstand,
Disintegrating jalousies,
Summer rain coming in on the tiles,

A desk, a high armchair,
Garish towels,
A bed in the corner
With white counterpane,
Edged with leaves and tiny roses.

Boat

Take the small boat
From its moorings in the field.
Let it bring you by trimmed banks,

Where ducks plop heavily onto water,
Through havens of secretive swans
And leafy stretches where blithe birds sing.

Do not fear,
Even when night falls and you sleep,
Even when rain lambastes the plain.

Through the valleys of doubt,
The gullies of uncertainty,
It will carry you still.

Riverbed

Quite suddenly that Summer,
The water drained from the river.
The rounded cobbles of the riverbed
Glistered in the light.
We could walk dryshod,

Discovering trees we had never noticed,
Clumps of broom and fern,
Pools with cornucopia of slithery trout
We could lift without nets
From the water.

Pool

I never reached the pool
In the inlet over the rocks:
Fear of an incoming tide
And clouds mustering on the sun
Made me clamber back the cliff.

So I can only imagine
Its clarity and cold,
The ribbons of torn wrack,
Shells disintegrating into sand,
The shock of its water on my skin.

Todi

Deep under the bright squares of the city,
Cold water rests, unlit,
In douce cisterns.

Men like we are—
Hopeful once. Sinful. Temples of God's Spirit—
Lived their lives here, digging.

Their ghosts leave no trace on the air.

Frost

Through the years of unpitying heat,
He dreamt of such mornings:

Trees bare,
The world at rest;

And his withered heart
Touched to life by frost.

Forgetfulness

The rivulets of memory
Trickle out to nothingness.

Mostly now,
He is seeking a waterpool of his past
Where children play raucously.

Faces, once familiar,
Gaze at him with unsought solicitude.

He fumes against confinement.
He frets for somebody,
Falsely accused.

He packs and repacks his suitcase
But cannot tell
Where he must urgently go.

Someone plays hide and seek
With his meagre treasures.
Somebody has stolen his last kobo.

What does he murmur,
Sitting in the bareness of prayer,
To that forgetful God, forgetting him?

Look, Lord!

For days now,
The frost is over everything.
In his bed, he prays without ceasing,
Fingering his beads
With his one sound hand.

He is caught helplessly in his body:
His mind is dark,
Even as melting frost
Falls from naked trees
Like raindrops in the sun.

Recovery

Our helpless watch is done,
Our questioning of Almighty Love's benevolence.
Already your crass demands fade in memory.
We can talk again of old kindnesses, wit, acuity:
All that made you lovable and loved.

Widower

He wanders through the house, uncomforted.
His collar takes on a sheen of matted grime.
His shirt is lustreless.

Cups and jars go back no longer
To their presses.
There is crackle of sugar under the plates.

He waits for a knock,
A phone,
An unheralded visitor.

As he mounts to his room,
Seeking some disremembered thing,
The window on the stairwell throws meagre light.

The Home

Now that the body has been removed
And the last tuts are tutted,
They return to the everyday of ache and ailment,
Unrattled by death.

Someone else takes the empty bed,
The place at table, the seat by the window.
Fresh batches of visitors
Hesitate through the doorway.

Winter Funeral

The funeral was in Winter,
Without chant or music.

Afterwards, we walked into the frost.
Our footsteps crunched on gravel.

Trees were white and gaunt.
A hapless pheasant crossed our path.

Prayers accomplished, we moved away,
Brushing death from our coats.

Mia

1.

The doors slide shut
Just as we reach the platform;
And the tram moves off into morning.

We glimpse you, for a second,
Waving slightly, laughing,
Decked for a Summer occasion.

How can we grudge you
To the territory of light?

2.

You would not, I know,
Have us make furious commotion
At your death;

Remember instead
Eyes sparkling with mirth,
Your loveliness, your panache;

Mostly,
How you knelt before the afflicted
To wash their aching feet.

3.

You sit deep into your chair,
Holding an enormous bouquet.
People crowd around you,
Celebrating something we do not understand.

4.

You are at a small table outside a restaurant
On a green hill above a city,
Gesturing us to join you.

We have come out only now
From airless corridors.
We hurry to you mirthfully,

Knowing we have reached,
Where you are,
Some bastion of changeless joy.

5.

You were there early and smiling.
You wanted to be sure they had forgotten nothing:
The wine, the meats, the fruity sorbets.

You led us through narrow streets
To where the tables were set,
Under awnings, in the glitter of the sea.

We had all grown older.
We talked rapidly
To ward against the fragility of the dream.

Reverie

It is a sheer drop from the walls
To the allotments,
Where women are tying vines to trellises
And men are digging black lines on the earth.
Birds fly effortlessly between.

Your ravaged body relinquished,
I know you are but a leaf-rustle away,
Breathing new air,
Wiping awestruck eyes awake,
Luxuriating in the clemency of sun.

Kieran

Drowned in Clonea, 22.8.1976, Aged 10

At times we dreamt of you,
Grown to manhood,
Taking possession of a gilt and waiting world.

Your mind was a glistering thing:
You could reel the names
Of brontosaurs and dinosaurs

And a hundred Mesozoic beasts
I still have no tag on.
Your face was perfect as Meissen.

You were all the future
Two small people hoped for
Until that day

When the deceitful sea
Slinked over sand
To conquer them.

Mourning a Father

A year later,
Sitting in a vast square
In a warm country,

Listening to a fountain
Gurgle and spill,
Watching it gather

And scatter the light,
Suddenly I unloose
The tears of my loss.

Two children stop their play
To regard my strangeness,
Too young yet to know

How loss and sorrow
Lie low to break us.

Mourning a Mother

When we were dismantling your bed,
After you died,
Out from nowhere
Dropped the old glass rosary beads,
You had scoured the house for.

They were the chain you tugged
To summon heavenly attention.
I finger them now,
Futilely,
To find heaven, to find you.

The Deaths of Parents

After he died,
I knew that he was still
Benevolently about me.

Something in a sky,
A flower,
A shadow crossing,

A banal salvation
No one else might comprehend,
Assured me.

Years later,
When she went,
I found only a grey and looming wall

That neither trust
Nor imagination
Could take me over.

Parenting

for my father

Not until your grandchildren grew tall
Could I understand
How we were treasured,

How you would have planned together,
As she readied you for road,
Beyond ambulance and clinic,

To those meetings
When I would walk along the canal
After classes

To find you waiting,
Arms stretched,
Eager for my trivia.

I thank you now, in retrospect,
For that
Which I had no power then to comprehend.

Growing Away

You brought us on your bike,
One on the bar and one behind,
To a sandy inlet of the ocean.

We ran wildly
To reach the outspreading waves,
Pushing,

Against your strictures,
Towards farther and farther,
Sunblessed breakers

Eily

She was at the long table,
Rolling pastry for tarts.
Her mother, dressed in widow's black,
Was on the chair by the fire,
Watching over a bastible roast.

A portrait of Emmet hung over the fireplace.
The china in the cabinet
Linked them to all their foremothers.
A red dog stretched itself lengthways
Along the floor.

The door to the yard was open.
A rosegarden separated them
From the cattle.
Hens cackled behind wire.
Calves lowed from the field.

I played with an indolent cat,
Grew bored,
Took out the vivid photograph book,
Not knowing then how I would treasure
The ordinariness of such days.

Birds

1.

We are sustained by dream,
Even in blackness.
Here where a hawk has swooped,
White feathers stir in the sun.

2.

Frost in April, disappearing
Already in the light:
Ducks waddle to water,
Pigeons pick the lawn.

3.

Easter again: the bare trees
Are uttering their first soft leaves.
Something prepotent drives the blackbird:
Its wet beak filled with straw.

4.

Ducks skid to water,
The hedges fill with song.
A fallen blackbird
Lies like an affront on the grass.

5.

The swans move lazily,
Keeping their own counsel:
They have dipped their necks
In the ponds of eternity.

6.

Earlier and earlier
A morning bird awakens me:
From the timing of its song,
I measure the stretching of days.

7.

A solitary thrush is singing,
Letting its rivals know, even as light creeps in,
That it is lord of its bush.
One by one, the other birds awake, like sleeptalkers, murmuring.

8.

A weary heron alights magnificently on a city gate,
High over our travail,
In a while, it will lift again,
Its eye on shimmering waterways beyond our view.

9.

The herons have found an island
In a lake, in a park, in a city
With trees to hang on,
Untidily as rags at a well.

10.

Early morning and already the swallows are finding feasts in the sky.
Pigeons plunder the remains of last night's roistering.
At a bus shelter near the sea, two lost humans cling to each other,
Cling.

11.

A pheasant stands on a headland,
Attentive to every move and murmur of the field,
Unaware that, all around, creation is agasp
Before its own red quiddity.

12.

The sun makes its way kindly
Through the trees,
Creating glittering light-pools on the track.
A robin flits from bush to bush.

13.

It is the final frame.
The hired killers are dead.
All is quiet. A bird sings.
The man walks, in long boots, wearily into sunset.

Winter Day

A fox has been across the snow
Before dawn.
The skeletal thorn in the field
Has taken on white beauty.
The small birds are invisible.

A skinny pigeon,
Exhausted in battle,
Lands on a forecourt,
Prey, after its striving,
To dog or cat or random stalking thing.

Praise

No wind ruffles the leaves
Of Autumn trees,
Birds are busy
Claiming their branches;

And this bothered, sceptic heart
Lifts again to praise
Whatever God or Accident
Sent first the atoms hurtling.

Lovebirds

Moorhens, busy as ants,
Run back and forward
Over an ice-locked lake.

Gulls, dropping barely a crumb,
Fight in the air for slices of bread
A child has scattered.

Islanded geese mutter against
The thawed space left for them to sport in.
Ducks plop to water.

Gloves on a wire fence
Lean into one another
Like lovebirds.

Owl

Its soft feathers achieve a silence
That barely disturbs the dark.
Its body, in between its outspread wings,
Is a fluffy thing a child might cuddle,

Not knowing that all this quiet
Covers a heart ordained
To search for small lives in the night,
To swoop and kill.

Fionn's Singer

A tall ship rises out of the dark,
Heavy with cargo:
Barrels of frozen raspberries,
Casks of apples, casks of nuts,

Cloth of silver, cloth of gold,
A bird in its cage,
Captured for its song.
We will free it into the oakwood.

Small Birds

1.

In a world alongside ours,
The small birds find their patches,
Picking at the drifted seed of urban grasses,
Discovering banquets in bins,
Feasts in rubble.

Some lift and fall in squabbling packs,
Most go singly about,
Unobserved,
Warily watching
At the corners of our lives.

2.

The enclaves of the rich
Cannot exclude them
Nor the citadels of the powerful.

They pick at the waste of the afflicted,
Shake down dandelion seed
In prison yards.

We are creatures of parallel life,
Interrupting their sway,
Demanding routine vigilance.

Starlings

Leaving smoke and noise behind,
I mount the steps
Into a car-less square, steeped in sunlight:

Soft stone, a patch of burnt grass
And a single bush
Alive with starlings,

Cheeping busily to one another
About something immense.

Lightning Source UK Ltd.
Milton Keynes UK
20 May 2010

154476UK00002B/32/P

9 781906 614201